WISDOM

Edited by
Margaret Neylon

Attic Press
Dublin

© Selection and editorial content Margaret Neylon 1992

All rights reserved. Except for brief passages quoted in newspaper, magazine, radio or television reviews, no part of this book may be reproduced in any form or by any means, electronic or mechanical, including photocopying or recording, or by any information storage and retrieval systems without prior permission in writing from the Publishers.

First published in 1992 by
Attic Press,
4 Upper Mount Street
Dublin 2

British Library Cataloguing in Publication Data
A catalogue record for this book is available from the British Library.

ISBN 1-85594-050-7

Cover Design: Kate White
Origination: Sinéad Bevan, Attic Press
Printing: Colour Books, Ltd, Dublin

MARGARET NEYLON lives in Dublin where she is Creative Director of an advertising agency. A short story writer and playwright, much of her work has been produced on radio. She is also author of *Pathways: A Source Book of Life Options* (Attic Press, 1991).

Attic Reflections Series

During the past few years we have seen an explosion of interest in the area generally referred to as 'New Age'. This can be seen in the enormous growth in the number of people taking an alternative approach to all aspects of living in the modern world.

The search for new alternatives reaches into the area of spirituality and personal development, with many seeking answers to questions of personal growth outside the more traditional methods.

In response to this need Attic Press is delighted to launch the **ATTIC REFLECTIONS SERIES**.

We will continue to add to this series with relevant and resourceful Reflections.

Beautifully presented and illustrated, these books will be ones you find yourself returning to again and again.

4

*How beautiful it is to do nothing,
and then to rest afterwards.*

Spanish Proverb

If you want a thing well done, get a couple of old broads to do it.

Bette Davis

Millions long for immortality who do not know what to do with themselves on a rainy Sunday afternoon.

Susan Ertz

The true secret of giving advice is, after you have honestly given it, to be perfectly indifferent whether it is taken or not and never persist in trying to set people right.

Hannah Whitall Smith

Lying is done with words and also with silence.

Adrienne Rich

When action grows unprofitable, gather information; when information grows unprofitable, sleep.

Ursula K Le Guin

The cock croweth but the hen delivereth the goods.

American Graffiti

When I am an old woman I shall wear purple
With a red hat which doesn't go, and doesn't suit me.
And I shall spend my pension on brandy and summer gloves
And satin sandals and say we've no money for butter.

       Jenny Joseph

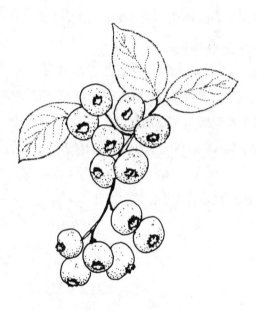

Success is counted sweetest by those who ne'er succeed.

Emily Dickinson

Language is magic: it makes things appear and disappear.
Nicole Brossard

As we reach midlife in the middle thirties or early forties, we are not prepared for the idea that time can run out on us, or for the startling truth that if we don't hurry to pursue our own definition of a meaningful existence, life can become a repetition of trivial maintenance duties.

Gail Sheehy

Painting changed me. Instead of feeling a hopeless muddle, inadequate in any given situation, doomed to be a misfit, an urgent purpose gave me direction. Using paint as a medium of transport, as it were, I had found a way to cast out my inner confusion.

Nicolette Devas

That's why we become witches: to show our scorn of pretending life's a safe business, to satisfy our passion for adventure ... to have a life of one's own, not an existence doled out to you by others.

                    Sylvia Townsend Warner

If you're small, you better be a winner.

Billie Jean King

By the time your life is finished, you will have learned just enough to begin it well.

                    Eleanor Marx

I've got two reasons for success and I'm standing on both of them.
                              Betty Grable

Beauty endures only for as long as it can be seen; goodness, beautiful today, will remain so tomorrow.

Sappho

Advice is what we ask for when we already know the answer but wish we didn't.

Erica Jong

I am, fundamentally, I think, an outsider. I do my best work and feel most braced with my back to the wall. It's an odd feeling, though, writing against the current: difficult entirely to disregard the current. Yet, of course, I shall.

Virginia Woolf

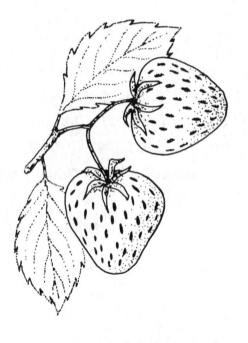

Integrity is so perishable in the summer months of success.

Vanessa Redgrave

Books, books, books. It was not that I read so much. I read and re-read the same ones. But all of them were necessary to me. Their presence, their smell, the letters of their titles, and the texture of their leather bindings.
                                Colette

Old age is not an illness, it is a timeless ascent. As power diminishes, we grow towards the light.

May Sarton

The only difference between a rut and a grave is their dimensions.

Ellen Glasgow

I got more children than I can rightly take care of, but I ain't got more than I can love.

Ossie Guffy

Whenever I have to choose between two evils, I always like to try the one I haven't tried before.

Mae West

Some people talk simply because they think sound is more manageable than silence.

Margaret Halsey

Once you find your voice you know that you can never be passively silent again. Your spur to creation is the desire to communicate. To have a meaningful exchange with other people in order to develop yourself, and therefore your work, even further. So much, yet so little time? The only answer is DO IT NOW!

Maud Sulter

If sex is such a natural phenomenon, how come there are so many books on how to?

       Bette Midler

Everyone has talent. What is rare is the courage to follow the talent to the dark place where it leads.

Erica Jong

Truth is so rare it's delightful to tell it.

Emily Dickinson

How do I know all this? Because I'm crazy. You can always trust the information given you by people who are crazy; they have an access to truth not available through regular channels.

                                         Norma Jean Harris

Adornment is never anything except a reflection of the heart.

Coco Chanel

The art of being an artist, if you weren't born in the right place, is to be able to live through rejections. A lot of them. To be able to speak when silenced. To be able to hear when not being heard. To be able to see and make seen when no one looks.

Gabriela Müller

All artists, in whatever medium, in fact work largely through the feminine side of their personalities. This is because works of art are essentially formed and created inside the mind of the maker, and are hardly at all dependent on external circumstances.

Joan Riviere

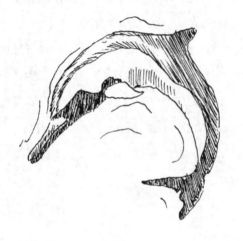

I think democracy takes time. The benefits are so high the voice of every woman counts, and counts equally, and even though it costs time and even though we have to cope with a little chaos sometimes because of it, it is worth it.

Sigmunden Kristansdottir

*Learning moment by moment to be free
in our minds and hearts, we make freedom possible for everyone the world over.*

Sonia Johnson

If truth is beauty, how come no one has their hair done in the library?
                              Lily Tomlin

There's a period of life when we swallow a knowledge of ourselves and it becomes either good or sour inside.

                                                   Pearl Bailey

By the time you say you're his
Shivering and sighing
And he vows his passion is
Infinite, undying -
Lady, make a note of this
One of you is lying.

Dorothy Parker

I'm working so hard on my time management that I don't get anything done.

Rose Johnston

Difficulties, opposition, criticism - these things are meant to be overcome, and there is a special joy in facing them and in coming out on top. It is only when there is nothing but praise that life loses its charm, and I begin to wonder what I should do about it.

Vijaya Lakshmi Pandit

Bitterness is like cancer. It eats upon the host. But anger is like fire. It burns it all clean.

Maya Angelou

I'll keep my personal dignity and pride to the very end - it's all I have left and it's a possession that only myself can part with.

Daisy Bates

Anger as soon as fed is dead
'Tis starving makes it fat.
                    Emily Dickinson

Physical and mental energy come from feeling in control of your life, having real choices and being involved with others to find ways of organising for a change for the better.

Barbara Rogers

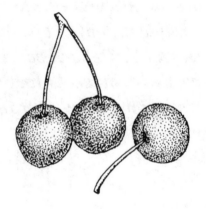

Erotic comes from the Greek word eros, the personification of love in all its aspects ... and personifying creative power and harmony. When I speak of the erotic, then, I speak of it as an assertion of the life force of women, of that creative energy empowered, the knowledge and use of which we are now reclaiming in our language, our history, our dancing, our loving, our work, our lives.

Audre Lord

If there had been no priesthood the world would have advanced ten thousand times better than it has now.

Annandabai Joshee

People pretend not to like grapes when they are too high for them to reach.

Marguerite de Navarre

The liar in her terror wants to fill up the void with anything. Her lies are a denial of her fear: a way of maintaining control.

Adrienne Rich

Only when one is no longer afraid to die is one no longer afraid at all. And only when we are no longer afraid do we begin to live in every experience, painful or joyous, to live in gratitude for every moment, to live abundantly.

       Dorothy Thompson

A slave is a person who is not paid for working. Sound familiar?

Astra

Who ever walked behind anyone to freedom? If we can't go hand in hand, I don't want to go.

Hazel Scott

Cleaning your house
While your kids are still growing
Is like shovelling the walk
Before it stops snowing.

Phyllis Diller

When we begin to take our failures less seriously, it means we are ceasing to be afraid of them. It is of immense importance to learn to laugh at ourselves.

       Katherine Mansfield

If I smiled or laughed, my helper did too. The universal language. This amazed me. I would have thought that tears were the things which bound us together, but no - smiles, laughter - and they warm up immediately.

Katherine Hepburn

The younger generation ... do not live in the present, they just live, as well as they can, and they do not plan. It is extraordinary that whole populations have no projects for the future, none at all. It certainly is extraordinary, but it is certainly true.

Gertrude Stein

Those who serve a cause are not those who love that cause. They are those who love the life which has to be led in order to serve it... and they are rare.

— Simone Weil

I'm an Irish Catholic and I have a long iceberg of guilt.

Edna O'Brien

If you don't like my ocean
Don't fish in my sea
Stay out of my valley
And let my mountains be!

                                      Ma Rainey

In the face of an obstacle which is impossible to overcome, stubbornness is stupid.

Simone de Beauvoir

I had never been as resigned to ready-made ideas as I was to ready-made clothes, perhaps because, although I couldn't sew, I could think.

Jane Rule

Creative minds have always been known to survive any kind of bad training.

Anna Freud

Spring is here, and I could be very happy, except that I am broke.
                    Edna St Vincent Millay

If you have never been hated by your child, you have never been a parent.
Bette Davis

*To be with you, my love,
is not at all like being in heaven
but like being in the earth.*

                                        Moya Cannon

You can take no credit for beauty at sixteen. But if you are beautiful at sixty, it will be your soul's own doing.

Marie Stopes

My consciousness is fine. It's my pay that needs raising.

Sharon Maledy

When a small child ... I thought that success spelled happiness. I was wrong, happiness is like a butterfly which appears and delights us for one brief moment, but soon flits away.

Anna Pavlova

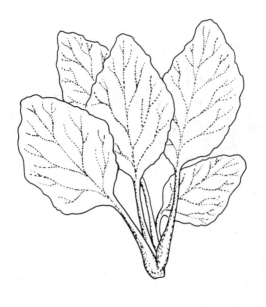

I refuse to believe that trading recipes is silly. Tuna fish casserole is at least as real as corporate stock.
Barbara Grizzuti

The art of writing is the art of applying the seat of the pants to the chair.

Mary Heaton-Vorse

But everybody needs a home so at least you can have some place to leave, which is where most other folks will say you must be coming from.

June Jordan

Rare and fortunate days these, for you reach the top of the slope and wake up, almost refreshed ... Do you dream because you are walking so easily? Or do you walk so easily because you dream?

Dorothy Pilley

To inspire is to draw air into the lungs - to be inspiring is to breathe life and dreams and have them become real.

Carmen Silva

I have not labelled myself yet. I would like to call myself revolutionary, for I am always changing, and growing, it is hoped for the good of more black people. I do call myself black when it seems necessary to call myself anything.
                                    Alice Walker

Give me a dozen such heartbreaks if that would help me lose a couple of pounds.

Colette

If I had my life to live again, I'd make the same mistakes, only sooner.
  Tallulah Bankhead

Opinions differ most when there is least scientific warrant for having any.

Daisy Bates

Life is a slate where all our sins are written; from time to time we rub the sponge of repentance over it so we can begin sinning again.

— George Sand

I don't want to get to the end of my life and find that I just lived the length of it. I want to have lived the width of it as well.

       Diane Ackerman

All the privilege I claim for my own sex ... is that of loving longest, when existence or hope is gone.

Jane Austen

What a wonderful life I've had! I only wish I'd realised it sooner.

Colette

One reason I don't drink is that I want to know when I am having a good time.

Nancy Astor

Recovery is a process, not an event.
         Anne Wilson Schaef

I enjoy life because I am endlessly interested in people and their growth. My interest leads me continually to widen my knowledge of people, and this in turn compels me to believe that the normal human heart is born good.

Pearl S Buck

*Why is it no one ever sent me yet
One perfect limousine, do you suppose?
Ah no, it's always just my luck to get one perfect rose.*

       Dorothy Parker

*I wish I'd a knowed more people.
I would of loved 'em all. If I'd a
knowed more, I woulda loved more.*
Toni Morrison

Perhaps we unconsciously avoid situations for which we are ill-equipped, even if avoiding them entails an amount of immediate suffering.

Dervla Murphy

None of the fifteen legal men, comprising judge, senior and junior barristers and solicitors had ever witnessed childbirth. 'Is it possible,' the judge was to ask 'for a woman to give birth standing up?' Women have given birth under water, in aeroplanes, in comas, lying unnaturally flat on their backs in hospital beds and even after death, but this man wondered if they could do it standing up ... .

Nell McCafferty

Never eat anything at one sitting that you can't lift.

Miss Piggy

Of course I am shocked by his death. But not nearly as shocked as when he walked out on me.

Sophie Levene

Riches do not always score,
Loving words are better far.
Just one helpful act is more
Than a gaudy motor car.
Happy thoughts contentment bring
Crabbed millionaires can't know;
Money doesn't mean a thing -
Try to tell the butcher so!

                          Dorothy Parker

Wealth without virtue
*   is a harmful companion*
but a mixture of both,
*   the happiest friendship.*
*   Sappho*

How do you like what you have? This is a question that anybody can ask anybody. Ask it.

Gertrude Stein

Some people are more turned on by money than they are by love. In one respect they're alike. They're both wonderful as long as they last.

Abigail Van Buren

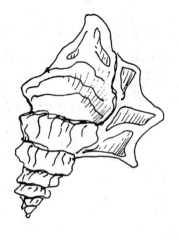

Motherhood is the most emotional experience of one's life. One joins a kind of women's mafia.

       Janet Suzman

One cannot live well, love well or sleep well unless one has dined well.
Virginia Woolf

I'm not against mothers. I am against the ideology which expects every woman to have children, and I'm against the circumstances under which mothers have to have their children.

Simone de Beauvoir

My mother was a brilliant person. She came second to nobody. She was the rock of the family ... She would never, never, never give up.

Corine Lytle Cannon

In search of my mother's garden I found my own.

Alice Walker

Wanna fly, you have to give up the shit that weighs you down.

Toni Morrison

The shortest answer is doing.
English Proverb

Too often, the opportunity knocks, but by the time you push back the chain, push back the bolt, unhook the two locks and shut off the burglar alarm, it's too late.

Rita Coolidge

When I feel physically as if the top of my head were taken off, I know that is poetry.

Emily Dickinson

I do want to get rich but I never want to do what there is to do to get rich.

Gertrude Stein

Happiness is good health and a bad memory.

Ingrid Bergman

And what a delight it is to make friends with someone you have despised.

Colette

I'm not going to limit myself just because people won't accept the fact that I can do something else.

Dolly Parton

Put a little fun in your life - try dancing.

Kathryn Murray

We are people at the bottom of the mountain struggling to go up and saying to those in power who are at the top: 'Come down, meet us halfway so that we can live and share and be together.' And the longer they delay coming down [...] well, we are coming up, and the harder they will fall when they finally tumble down.

                        Motlalepula Chabaku

I was taught that the way of progress is neither swift nor easy.

Marie Curie

There is really nothing more to say - except why. But since why is difficult to handle, one must take refuge in how.

Toni Morrison

When nothing is sure, everything is possible.

Margaret Drabble

Make it a rule of life never to regret and never look back. Regret is an appalling waste of energy; you can't build on it; it is good only for wallowing in.

                                     Katherine Mansfield

The only thing you ever have any control of is your current thought. Your old thoughts have gone, there is nothing you can do about them except live out the experiences they caused. Your future thoughts have not been formed, and you do not know what they will be. Your current thought, the one you are thinking right now, is totally under your control.

Louise L Hay

Until you've lost your reputation you never realise what a burden it is, or what freedom really is.

Margaret Mitchell

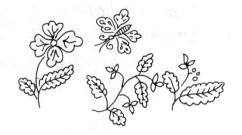

*If love makes the world go round, then
why are we going to outer space?*
                              Margaret Gilman

The happy people are failures because they are on such good terms with themselves that they don't give a damn.

> Agatha Christie

One loses many laughs by not laughing at oneself.

Sara Duncan

I feel like I'm fighting a battle when I didn't start a war.

Dolly Parton

At fifteen life had taught me undeniably that surrender, in its place, was as honourable as resistance, especially if one had no choice.

Maya Angelou

*You say I am mysterious
Let me explain myself
In a land of oranges
I am faithful to apples.*

                                         Elsa Gidlow

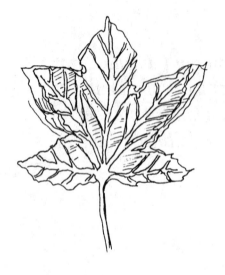

One doesn't recognise in one's life the really important moments - until it's too late.

Agatha Christie

Don't compromise yourself. You're all you've got.

Janice Joplin

Women who set a low value on themselves make life hard for all women.

      Nellie McClung

Make the most of every sense: glory in all the facets of pleasure and beauty which the world reveals to you through the several means of contact which nature provides. But of all the senses, sight must be the most delightful.

— *Helen Keller*

There is nothing new except that which is forgotton.

Mademoiselle Bertin

In fact, it's quite ridiculous, the shapes people throw when they get down to it. There are few positions more ridiculous - to look at - than the positions people adopt when they are together. Limbs everywhere. Orifices gaping. Mucus pouring out and in. Sweat flying. Sheets wrecked. Animals and insects fleeing the scene when the going gets rough. Noise? My dear, the evacuation of Dunkirk in World War Two was an intellectual discussion compared to it. Once in a while, of course, there's silence. Usually afterwards. It's called exhaustion.

Nell McCafferty

The two most beautiful words in the English language are 'cheque enclosed'.

Dorothy Parker

When I am writing, I allow myself small ritualised pleasures as breaks from the writing-pleasures. The cup of herbal tea, bright light, luxury of the fan heater for half an hour. Tidying the workplace, because that's part of the work. A few minutes stretching or dancing, because the body is part of it.

        Helen Mc Neil

Success to me is having ten honeydew melons and eating only the top half of each.

Barbra Streisand

You grow up the day you have your first real laugh - at yourself.

Ethel Barrymore

See
No matter what you have done
I am still here,
And it has made me dangerous, and wise.
And brother,
You cannot whore, perfume and suppress me any more.
I have my own business in this skin
And on this planet.

Gail Murray

The best way to keep children home is to make the atmosphere happy - and let the air out of the tyres.

      Dorothy Parker

I believe talent is like electricity. We do not understand electricity. We use it. Electricity makes no judgement. You can plug into it, and light up a lamp, keep a heart pump going, light a cathedral, or you can electrocute a person with it ... I think talent is like that. I believe every person is born with talent.

Maya Angelou

It takes nothing more than an addition, subtraction and a gift for deceit to balance a cheque book.

        Kendall Hailey

Your mind is a tool for you to use in any way you wish. The thoughts you choose to think create the experiences you have. Do not think your mind is in control. You are in control of your mind.

Louise L Hay

Contrary to popular belief, English women do not wear tweed nightgowns.

Hermione Gingold

Pain is the root of knowledge.
　　　　　　　　　　Simone Weil

Too often travel, instead of broadening the mind, merely lengthens the conversation.

       Elizabeth Drew

The only thing I like about rich people is their money.

Nancy Astor

I am pure as the driven slush.
　　　　　　　　Tallulah Bankhead

People that keep stiff upper lips find that it's damn hard to smile.

                                                  Judith Guest

The common woman is as common as the best bread and will rise.

Judy Grahn

When a lion emerges from the forest, no one bothers to ask whether it is male or female.

Ruth Vanita

Flowers grow out of dark moments.
                              Corita Kent

The best careers advice to give the young is, find out what you like doing best and get someone to pay you for doing it.

        Katherine Whilehaen

Keep in mind always the present you are constructing. It should be the future you want.

Alice Walker

Keyword Index

Adornment 67
Adventure 29
Advice 11, 39, 295
Afraid 103, 111
Anger 87, 91
Animals 257
Artist 69, 71
Avoid 177

Beautiful 5
Beauty 37, 77, 135, 253
Begin 33
Birth 179
Bitterness 87
Black 151
Books 45, 59
Brandy 19
Bread 289
Broads 7

Career 295
Catholic 119
Cause 117
Change 93, 151
Chaos 73
Childbirth 179
Children 51, 109, 131, 197, 269
Choice 93, 243
Cleaning 109

Cock 17
Common 289
Communicate 57
Compromise 249
Confusion 29
Consciousness 137
Control 93, 101, 231
Conversation 281
Courage 61
Crazy 65
Creative 57, 127
Credit 135
Criticism 85

Dancing 219
Dangerous 267
Dark 293
Death 103, 179, 183
Deceit 273
Democracy 73
Develop 57
Difficulty 85
Dignity 89
Dream 147, 149
Drink 167

Earth 133
Energy 93, 95, 229
English 259, 277
Erotic 95

Evils 53
Exhaustion 257
Existence 25
Experience 231, 275

Failures 111
Fear 101
Fighting 241
Flowers 293
Freedom 75, 107, 233
Friend 187, 215
Fun 219
Future 115, 231, 297

Goodness 37
Grapes 99
Grave 49
Growth 151, 171
Guilt 119

Happiness 129, 139, 237, 269
Hate 131
Heart 67, 75
Heartbreak 153
Hen 17
Home 145
Hope 163
Human 171

Ideas 125
Immortality 9

Information 15
Inspire 149
Integrity 43
Irish 119

Knowledge 79, 279

Language 23, 95, 113
Laugh 111, 113, 239, 265
Law 179
Learning 75
Liar 101
Life 33, 165, 171
Limit 217
Lion 291
Live 69, 103, 115, 117, 155, 161, 195, 221, 231, 247
Love 51, 95, 117, 133, 191, 195, 235
Lying 13, 81, 179

Memory 213
Midlife 25
Mind 75, 127, 275
Mistakes 155
Money 19, 185, 191, 259, 273, 283, 295
Motherhood 193, 197, 201
Mothers 197
Mysterious 245

Nature 253
New 255
Nothing 5

Obstacle 123
Old 7, 19, 47, 231
Opinions 157
Opportunity 207
Opposition 85
Outsider 41

Pain 279
Parent 131
Pleasure 253
Poetry 209
Positions 257
Possible 227
Priesthood 97
Progress 223
Pure 285

Refuge 225
Regret 229
Repentance 159
Reputation 233
Revolutionary 151
Riches 185
Rise 289

Shit 203
Sight 253
Silence 257
Slave 105

Sleep 195
Slush 285
Smile 287
Soul 135
Spring 129
Struggling 221
Stubbornness 123
Success 21, 35, 43, 139, 263
Suffering 177
Surrender 243

Talent 61, 271
Talk 55
Think 125
Travel 281
Tweed 277

Value 251
Voice 57, 73

War 241, 257
Wealth 187
Wish 39, 165, 175, 275
Witches 29
Woman 19, 73, 95, 179, 193, 197, 289, 251, 277
Work 2 61
Writing 41, 143, 261

Youth 115

300

Author Index

Ackerman, Diane 161
American Graffiti 17
Angelou, Maya 87, 243, 271
Astor, Nancy 167, 283
Astra 105
Austen, Jane 163

Bailey, Pearl 79
Bankhead, Tallulah 155, 285
Barrymore, Ethel 265
Bates, Daisy 89, 157
Bergman, Ingrid 213
Bertin, Mademoiselle 255
Brossard, Nicole 23
Buck, Pearl S 171

Cannon, Moya 133
Chabaku, Motlalepula 221
Chanel, Coco 67
Christie, Agatha 237, 247
Colette 45, 153, 165, 215
Coolidge, Rita 207
Curie, Marie 223

Davis, Bette 7, 131

de Beauvoir, Simone 123, 197
de Navarre, Marguerite 99
Devas, Nicolette 27
Dickinson, Emily 21, 63, 91, 209
Diller, Phyllis 109
Drabble, Margaret 227
Drew, Elizabeth 281
Duncan, Sara 239

English Proverb 205
Ertz, Susan 9

Freud, Anna 127

Gidlow, Elsa 245
Gilman, Margaret 235
Gingold, Hermione 277
Glasgow, Ellen 49
Grable, Betty 35
Grahn, Judy 289
Grizzuti, Barbara 141
Guest, Judith 287
Guffy, Ossie 51

Hailey, Kendall 273
Halsey, Margaret 55
Harris, Norma Jean 65

Hay, Louise L 231, 275
Heaton-Vorse, Mary 143
Hepburn, Katherine 113

Johnson, Sonia 75
Johnston, Rose 83
Jong, Erica 39, 61
Joplin, Janice 249
Jordan, June 145
Joseph, Jenny 19
Joshee, Annandabai 97

Keller, Helen 253
Kent, Corita 293
King, Billie Jean 31
Kristansdottir, Sigmunden 73

Lakshmi Pandit, Vijaya 85
Le Guin, Ursula K 15
Levene, Sophie 183
Lord, Audre 95
Lytle Cannon, Corine 199

McCafferty, Nell 179, 257
McClung, Nellie 251
Mc Neil, Helen 261
Ma Rainey 121

Maledy, Sharon 137
Mansfield, Katherine 111, 229
Marx, Eleanor 33
Midler, Bette 59
Miss Piggy 181
Mitchell, Margaret 233
Morrison, Toni 175, 203, 225
Müller, Gabriela 69
Murphy, Dervla 177
Murray, Gail 267
Murray, Kathryn 219

O'Brien, Edna 119

Parker, Dorothy 81, 173, 185, 259, 269
Parton, Dolly 217, 241
Pavlova, Anna 139
Pilley, Dorothy 147

Redgrave, Vanessa 43
Rich, Adrienne 13, 101
Riviere, Joan 71
Rogers, Barbara 93
Rule, Jane 125

Sand, George 159
Sappho 37, 187
Sarton, May 47
Scott, Hazel 107

Sheehy, Gail 25
Silva, Carmen 149
Spanish Proverb 5
St Vincent Millay, Edna 129
Stein, Gertrude 115, 189, 211
Stopes, Marie 135
Streisand, Barbra 263
Sulter, Maud 57
Suzman, Janet 193

Thompson, Dorothy 103
Tomlin, Lily 77
Townsend Warner, Sylvia 29

Van Buren, Abigail 191
Vanita, Ruth 291

Walker, Alice 151, 201, 297
Weil, Simone 117, 279
West, Mae 53
Whitehaen, Katherine 295
Whitall Smith, Hannah 11
Wilson Schaef, Anne 169
Woolf, Virginia 41, 195

If you have any suggestions for subjects you would like see in the *Attic Reflections Series* or any quotes which you particularly like.
Please write to us at:
Attic Press,
4 Upper Mount Street,
Dublin 2